Stick insects, stick bugs and pets.

A Complete owner's guide.

Care, facts, costs, food, handling, cages, health, breeding and where to buy all included.

by

Elliott Lang

Published by IMB Publishing 2014

Table of Contents

Table of Contents

Introduction

Stick insects are just such lovely creatures, both in the wild and as pets. Being varied in size, shape and colour depending on the species, you might even find yourself joining the ranks of collectors who keep, breed and display a vast array of stick insects from all over the world, with their exotic beauty making quite a talking point, not only with other phasmid enthusiasts.

As with all exotic pets, stick insects have specific food and environmental needs and require special care and attention in order to live happily and healthily in captivity. In order to keep stick insects as pets you need to have a good understanding of their needs and any problems that could arise.

Stick insects can make wonderful pets to the right people and with the right preparation stick insects can be very happy in captivity. They require very little in the way of stimulation and enrichment and get on very well with only each other for company. This book will look at everything you need to know when making your decision of whether or not to keep these sweet little creepy crawlies. It will go through all of their requirements and the possible pitfalls of keeping stick insects.

If you do decide you want a stick insect, this book can help you prepare for your new arrival and preparation is key. The wellbeing of any animal in your care is your responsibility by law. This book aims to help you prepare for the arrival of your new stick insect.

As there are 3,000 types of stick insect and there is a wide base of knowledge that doesn't apply to all of them. There are 40 or so species that are kept in culture, and this book will tell you about the 20 or so that are most commonly kept and how to keep them. It will look at the specifics of each species in detail, and give you general information as well.

I absolutely love my lovely stick insects and I hope you will have just as much fun watching them as I do.

Chapter 1) Stick bugs, stick insects and leaf insects

There are so many differences between the various phasmids in culture that you wouldn't know they were related. Some of them are small and green and quite ordinary looking, others are stunning and big and can fly!

What we call stick bugs, stick insects and leaf insects are all phasmids of different shapes. They are not, as they might seem, different types of insect. Stick bug is another name for stick insect, and leaf insects are phasmids whose bodies are wider and flatter than the stick insects'. This makes the leaf insects very successful at camouflaging, and their stick insect cousins are equally good at blending into their background.

Perhaps no other group of insects is better named or easier to recognize than the order Phasmida. Phasmids use their unique camouflage to fool predators. With long legs and antennae, stick insects look so much like the twiggy bushes and tree branches where they spend their lives. Even the more flamboyant Achrioptera is able to hide as exotic branches or flatter and usually more colourful leaf insects resemble the foliage on which they feed.

Another reason people keep stick insects as pets, and that they make great pets for children, is that they are virtually free to keep. Once you've bought the stick insects wither as an adult for 50p-£5 or $1-9 depending on species, 10 eggs for that price, and the enclosure, which will cost anything from £5 or $9 to £80 or

$130, the cost of keeping them is virtually nothing. You need a piece of kitchen roll once a week and their food plants can be collected for nothing.

Stick insects can live (once hatched) from 8-24 months, but if you keep and hatch the eggs, you can keep a culture of them for decades.

The value of stick and leaf insects in education is greatly underrated. They allow a great deal of observation and investigation to be undertaken by students of all ages. Stick insects and leaf insects are incredibly well camouflaged insects of an order called Phasmidia. Phasmids are plant-eating insects that have evolved to look like their surroundings. They have 6 legs like all insects and are really fascinating little critters.

One of the reasons they are so popular as pets is that they are relatively easy to care for, needing fresh plant material to snack on, room to move about and a spray of water now and then. They don't need masses of space. The difficulty comes in perfecting the humidity, airflow and temperature that specific species require. Once you know what they need, though, they aren't much trouble at all. Unlike other insects that can be kept as pets, like Tarantulas, centipedes and mantids, they don't need live food.

As well as this, their short lifespan and rampant fecundity means you can watch their lifecycle over and over as eggs are laid and nymphs hatch and grow, shedding their skin like snakes as they grow, changing before your very eyes, from tiny little specks to beautiful, graceful creatures.

Of all the insects commonly kept as pets, stick insects are among the safest. They don't inject venom like tarantulas or centipedes, they don't shed noxious hairs, tarantulas again. They don't bite like a praying mantis might do if you wind it up – though some of the larger, more aggressive species might give you a little nip.

Some stick insects can be kept together in fabulous displays with potted plants in interesting cases. Collectors make truly beautiful cases and displays to show their phasmids in.

Collectors meet up at bug fairs and conventions and they talk on forums. In this new age of technology, information can be so easily shared and given. Because of this, phasmids are becoming more and more popular, and being kept more successfully than ever before.

Stick insects have been kept as pets and for scientific study for centuries, but people have also kept them for displays in zoological exhibitions.

Chapter 2) Choosing your stick insects

There are about 3,000 different types of stick and leaf insects in the world, but, realistically, there are only 300 or so types that are kept as pets, so that's well narrowed down already. After that, there are 20 or so interesting ones that you can easily get hold of and that do well in captivity throughout Europe and the United States.

The first thing you need to work out before you set your heart on a particular species are your needs and theirs. So there are some questions you should ask, and when you've got the answers, look at the species descriptions and choose who you want to take home!

Who are the stick insects for?

If you're an adult wanting an interesting addition to the collection or just a low maintenance pet then that doesn't narrow down the field much- they are all interesting and relatively low maintenance.

However, if they are for children, you might want to be careful. Some species are very delicate and can't be handled by children. Some are surprisingly spiky and sharp, with their hard exoskeleton being pinched into vicious barbs that can hurt little hands. And some excrete noxious chemicals that can do anything from making you sneeze to causing a horrid rash. One woman returned a pair of pink winged stick insects to me after she'd licked her hands after handling them and her mouth had gone numb.

If they are just for looking at, though, even children can't hurt themselves watching stick insects through the cage/tank.

There are some species of stick insect that have a poisonous defence mechanism, an incredible irritant that they spray when threatened. Peruvian black beauty (*Peruphasma schultei*) and, to a lesser extent, Pink Winged (*Sipyloidea sipylus*) and Peruvian Fern Stick insects (*Oreophoetes peruana*) do this, as do American Walking Sticks (*Anisomorpha bupestroides*). This can cause temporary blindness and considerable pain to an adult. It is very important you know the precise species of stick insect before you buy them. No spraying stick insects should be handled by children.

How much space do you have?

If you've not got masses of space to keep a large cage in, then you should consider only the smaller types that do not fly. If you've got lots of room, then the larger ones could suit you. Even the smaller, flying ones need space though, so if it flies, it needs to be in a bigger container.

What sort of food can you get hold of?

Most of the food for your stick insects can be taken from the garden or the roadside. Take a look at what might be available before getting stick insects that you can't feed.

Types of stick insects

Carausias morosus or Indian Stick Insects

Indian stick insects are most commonly kept as pets. The females are 8 times more common than the males, although they don't need males to reproduce. They are plain green and grow to about 3 inches long, with the males having red markings under the arms when the reach sexual maturity. They are easy to feed, they are easy to house and they reproduce readily, making them a cheep and easy choice for a first stick insect pets.

They are fairly interesting, but they don't move about as much as some other sticks, and they are quite plain looking.

Achrioptera

None of the Achrioptera are really suitable for children as their wings are very delicate. They do make fabulous display insects though, because not only are the beautiful, they are active in the day, so are great to watch. If you are confident that you can care for them, they do make much more interesting classroom displays than the common Indian stick insect.

Achrioptera punctipes cliquennoisi

The subtly beautiful Achrioptera punctipes cliquennoisi is, like it's cousins, a large flying stick insect that has a spinney body. The female is larger at up to 25cm, and is very pretty, though not as colourful. The male is smaller, reaching up to 15cm. He has fantastic rainbow colours. They both have wings that are really

14

striking, with the females having orange and black markings while the males have black and orange wings with a red ridge.

These stick insects cannot be kept with smaller stick insects, as they could walk on them and push them off their holds. They also need a lot of room, due to both their size and their need for flying.

Achrioptera Fallax

The Achrioptera Fallax Stick Insect comes from Madagascar and is stunningly beautiful. The males are bright metallic blue and green and have a pair of red/orange spines along the top part of their legs. They have 2 pairs of wings, the front pair being bright yellow and the back pair being red, with yellow and black markings. The females are brown, but still amazing to look at. Unlike Indian stick insects, the Achrioptera Fallax Stick Insect needs both male and female to reproduce. The male can grow up to 13cm, and the larger female up to 18cm.

While these are much more exotic looking, they are more difficult and expensive to get hold of and need more space per insect as not only are they much larger, but without gliding space, their wings can become damaged.

Achrioptera Punctipes Punctipes

A close relative of Achrioptera Fallax, the Achrioptera Punctipes Stick Insect is equally exotic and beautiful. The males are slightly greener than those of the Achrioptera Fallax, though they are very similar in size, and the legs are a golden colour.

The wings are bigger and fully developed, whereas the Achrioptera Fallax has 'bud' wings. And these wings are beautiful. They have blackish bluish shades with green and red at the ridge and they have red antennae. The female of this species is very large, reaching up to 22cm long; she is one of the larger stick insect species. She has blue hints on her brown, spiny body.

These are very beautiful, but need much more space than the smaller stick insects and will need flying room. They are also harder and more expensive to buy.

Acrophylla Wuelfingi

The much plainer Acrophylla Wuelfingi is another large, winged stick insect. The males are much smaller and more delicate looking. They have a pinkish brown colour, with some dusky green markings. The female is larger and her markings are more pronounced. She can reach up to 30cm.

Due to their spikes, these aren't really suitable for children. They also need a lot of space.

Diapherodes Gigantea

The Diapherodes Gigantea is an incredibly popular pet. The females are large, bright green and robust. They have fat bodies and legs and a nice big head. The males are much smaller, but they can fly! These guys are great for children as you can see their little feet and how they hang on, and their heads are obvious. They don't have any spines or secrete anything nasty either, so they are safe to handle. They are now relatively cheap to buy and feed.

The only down side with this species is that they need a lot of room to move about and to fly.

Borneo Giant Thorny Stick Insects

These guys look like something from Tolkien. They could have stepped right off the set of the hobbit. They are spiky little things and could be dried bramble sticks until they move. The male is much smaller than the female, but other than that they are fairly similar in appearance.

The only down side of these is their size, meaning they need a lot more room than smaller insects. Also, because these large sticks have spikes, they can't be handled by children.

17

Parapachymorpha zomproi

The Parapachymorpha zomproi is a great beginner's stick insect and great for children. They are broad and sturdy and they look like a dead stick. They are really easy to look after. They don't grow too big so can be kept in relatively small housing and they don't breed too veraciously, so it's difficult to get over run with them.

There are no real down sides to this stick insect. They are great!

Extatosoma Tiaratum

The Extatosoma Tiaratum, or Macleays Spectre is one of the larger species of stick insects that has been known to reach an adult size of 150mm. The females reach this size, but on average they reach 130mm. The females are wingless, only having small buds, whereas the males are fully winged and able to fly. The males are smaller than the females, averaging 90 - 100mm. Both sexes can range from light to medium brown, or a greenish colour. The females have lots of sharp spikes all over their body, but the males seem to be rather smooth. The legs are lobed and these too have small projections of spikes present.

They are very grumpy and aggressive. They can't be kept with other stick insects or handled by children.

Phaenopharos Khaoyaiens

The Phaenopharos Khaoyaiensis, or bug winged stick insects is very popular, as they are sturdy and don't grow too large. As the common name suggests, the wings of this species are only bud size and don't allow them to fly. This is an unusual species in that the males and females are very similar in size, shape and colour, the females growing to 14cm, with the males being only slightly smaller. They have dull, pale brown bodies with bright red wing buds that are often hidden away under black and beige casing.

They are easy enough to keep, but do need room as they can be quite active.

Ramulus nematodes Blue

The rare and beautiful Ramulus nematodes Blue is much sought after by collectors, but you can get hold of them as eggs to hatch. They are extremely delicate and fine. The female is well camouflaged, being a green or sandy colour. But the male! He is striking metallic blue with darker legs. These are fairly easy to keep and the eggs are cheap enough, but they don't hatch as readily as other species.

The main problem with these is that they are too delicate for children to handle at all and even adults must be extremely careful – they are gossamer thin and you can barely feel them walking on your skin.

Peruphasma schultei

The Peruphasma schultei, or black beauty as they are sometimes called, is an odd looking thing. They have fat, flattish bodies with red bud wings. These are very pretty and easy to keep.

Unfortunately, they can excrete unpleasant chemicals when stressed, so they aren't really suitable for children.

Neohiasea maerens

Commonly known as the Vietnam Prickly stick insect, the Neohiasea maerens is a small, hairy looking stick insect that is very pretty to look at, easy to handle and a good insect to have around children.

The only down side with this species is that they can be quite hard to get hold of.

Asceles

The Thai Asceles stick insect is a stunning creature, with both males and females being fascinating to look at. The females are larger and redder than the males, who are greener. They both have wings and beautiful yellow markings. They are very easy to look after and they are much more lively than other species, moving about a lot.

The only problem here is that they can be hard to get hold of.

Heteropteryx dilatata or jungle nymph

The Heteropteryx dilatata or jungle nymph is a great display animal, as they are fat and interesting. The females of this species are very aggressive and much larger, wider, and brighter than the male. The female is lime green and has short, rounded wings, however their short length doesn't allow them to fly. The males are much smaller and a mottled brown colour. Both sexes have small spikes on their upper bodies, more numerous in the female, who also has very large spines on her hind legs that can snap together as a scissor-like weapon.

These are too aggressive to be handled by children or to live with other species.

Longhodes Philippinicus

The males are quite striking in appearance with orange and blue colour banding and grow to approximately 11cm. The females have the same banding but with 2 shades of green and reach 13cm. They don't fly or have wings.

Xenophasmina

These do not have wings at all. The females are sturdy phasmids that grow to about 10.5 - 12 cm and are different brown shades with 2 large spines (with green tips) on the Mesothorax. They also have many small, green humps on the body. The males are smaller, reaching about 7.5 - 8cm. The coloration is variable amongst males; there are light and dark specimens. Lightly coloured specimens are light brown with a brown-red, greenish-blue bordered area on the thorax.

Mearnsiana Bullosa

The Mearnsiana Bullosa are pretty little fat things, but not too long.

The females are very sturdy - about 9.5 cm long and fat! Their back is coloured in a strong green, brown-green or brown and their sides are coloured brownish, orange and purple.

The males are very interesting to look at, even though they are only 4-5cm. They are green and yellow and red and their thorax is chunky and lumpy.

Lopaphus Magnificus

The Lopaphus Magnificus is a nice little stick insect. The female will grow to 12-14cm and is yellow and pale green. The male is smaller, at 9-12cm, and is a very pretty. The green and yellow markings are more pronounced in the male. Neither of them has wings. They make good starter pets. They are easy to keep and to get hold of.

They aren't very interesting to look at though.

Cranidium Gibbosum

The males and females of this species are very different.

The females are big, bulky things, with their thorax and abdomen being strongly broadened - this gives them a somewhat leaf-like appearance. They are not very long compared to some of the other girls, with their body being 13 - 16 cm long. They are bright, light green or yellow-green on the top, and a dark green on the bottom. They have bumps on their backs.

The males are much thinner and shorter, being only 9 or so cm long. They are much brighter coloured, being bluish-green on the top, and a glossy green on the bottom and several brown and white areas. The males have fully developed wings to flutter for a shot distance.

They are easy enough to keep, but need a nice lot of space and food.

Neophasma subapterum

The Neophasma subapterum is another interesting looking stick. These are not as flamboyant as some of the other stick insects, but they have an unusual characteristic.

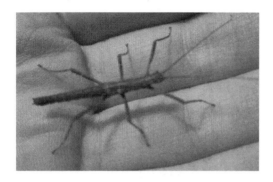

Where some stick insects have wings, these have little orange and yellow bud lumps. They are really interesting looking little guys. They are quite small, easy to keep and are relatively cheap.

The down side of these is that they are harder to get hold of as adults/ nymphs.

Eurycantha Calcarata

The Eurycantha Calcarata are fat, spiky brown and green little guys. Their bodies are like long, segmented beetles. None of them fly.

The females are larger than the males, as they often are, at 11-15 cm. They have an ovipositor at the end of their abdomen which kind of looks like a stinger but it is not used in defence.

The males only grow up to 11cm long and are grumpy little things.

These aren't good beginner phasmids, as the males have stabbing spikes on their hind legs and they snap their legs together hard, trapping anything that comes between these legs.

It can be very painful when it grabs your hand. They aren't recommended to be handled by children.

Tirachoidea Jianfenglingensis

The females of this species are big girls, growing to about 19 – 20 cm long. They are coloured in different red-brown shades and have 2 bumps behind their head – perhaps to confuse predators. Their long legs have many spines and they don't have wings.

The males are a fairly typical phasmid, growing to about 12 – 14 cm long and with their body and legs being mainly brown. Like the female, they have two distinct bumps on the back of their head. Unlike the females, the males are fully winged and can fly. The lateral area of the hind wings is a light green, like the rest of the body. The membranous part of hind wings (alae) is transparent, grey and with dark veins. They have spiky legs like the females.

Pharnacia kirbyi

The largest recorded stick insect is the Pharnacia kirbyi from Borneo, and it was 55cm. They are quite plain looking, distinguished mostly by their size. They are easy to feed if you can find their food where you live. They breed easily and live longer than most.

The main draw back of the Pharnacia kirbyi is that because of their size, they need very large cages.

Chapter 3) Stick insects in the wild

Despite their many similarities, the different types of stick insect are not found in the same places. Like lions and tigers, many of them would never meet in the wild. Unlike lions and tigers, stick insect types are not so closely related that they could interbreed. Even stick insects from the same countries would naturally behave differently and be found in different types of terrain. From observations of them in the wild, we can determine the conditions that would suit them best in captivity.

Stick and leaf insects live in forests or shrubby areas, requiring leaves and woody growth for food and protection. Worldwide, over 3,000 species belong to the order Phasmida. Entomologists describe just over 30 species in the United States and Canada.

Most insects in the order Phasmida, including all leaf insects, live in tropical climates. Phasmids are nocturnal feeders, so if you encounter one during the daytime, it will likely be resting.

Achrioptera

The species from Achrioptera are from Madagascar, where they live in the dense forests and are eaten by lots of mammals and birds. They are very beautiful and colourful, but this isn't, as you'd imagine, a disadvantage for them in hiding from predators. Their beautiful colours suggest that they are poisonous.

Acrophylla Wuflfingi

The handsome Australian Acrophylla Wuflfingi is another arboreal species that clamber about in the trees, hiding from the birds and mammals that prey on them.

Diapherodes Gigantea

The bold, chunky Diapherodes Gigantea comes from Caribbean islands and they spend much of their time eating and wandering about. Because of their size, they don't have many natural predators, so they are fairly calm in nature.

Parapachymorpha zomproi

In the wilds of Thailand, the handsome Parapachymorpha zomproi live in the trees and will occasionally hide under leaves on the ground.

Extatosoma Tiaratum insect

The wild behaviour of the vicious Macleay's spectre is fascinating. They lay eggs that look like large, edible seeds. Then, Leptomyrmex ants collect the seed-like eggs of Macleay's spectre and take them down to the foodstores.

Here they are kept in the humid, warm environment of the ant nest, and the ants keep them free from destructive fungi. Newly hatched nymphs mimic the ants, even running quickly. They look and smell so similar to the ants that they are out of harm's way within the nest until they can escape to the safety of the surface.

Phaenopharos Khaoyaiensis

The Phaenopharos Khaoyaiensis comes from Thailand, where they are nocturnal and hide well. They don't need much in the way of hiding places as they camouflage well.

Neophasma subapterum

In the wild, the Neophasma subapterum live both in the trees and on the ground. They are from Venezuela and are nocturnal.

Ramulus nematodes Blue

The stunning Ramulus nematodes Blue come from Thailand and are well adapted to the hot, humid climate.

Peruphasma schultei

The Peruvian black beauty is a stunning little thing, and in the wild they live on Schinus, a type of flowering tree. They are only known to exist in a region of less than 5 hectares there. They are equallyas comfortable in the day as they are at night, having excellent vision.

Neohiasea maerens

In the wild, the Neohiasea maerens live in Vietnam. They are nocturnal, and their showy spikes, though not functionally very dangerous, work well as a deterrent to predators.

Asceles

The beautiful Asceles live in Thailand, and like many other stick insects, they are nocturnal. They can also be found in Malaysia and Singapore.

Heteropteryx dilatata

Come from Malaysia and Borneo and live for up to 2 years. They are nocturnal. The Heteropteryx dilatata is a real little bruiser and defends itself viciously.

Longhodes Philippinicus

These phasmids are from the Philippines and are nocturnal. They are preyed upon by lots of birds and mammals, and they don't have much in the way of defensive behaviour.

Xenophasmina

The Xenophasmina come from Thailand and live on the bark of trees, where they blend in well.

Mearnsiana Bullosa

Coming from the Philippines, the Mearnsiana Bullosa clamber about in the twilight (early morning and evening). They live in the mountains.

Lopaphus Magnificus

Members of the Lopaphus Magnificus species are native to Vietnam and are nocturnal. They live on plants and are preyed on by almost everything!

Cranidium Gibbosum

They eat bramble, salal, buche and raspberry. They'll also eat oak too, if they are offered it in the summer.

Eurycantha Calcarata

This species is native to New Guinea. This species lives, in contrast to many other types of stick insects, on the ground and not in trees or bushes. They even hide under bark and stones during the daytime.

Tirachoidea Jianfenglingensis

There is relatively little known about these guys in the wild. Although they were first described in 1908, they have only recently been studied and collected. They have been found on Java, but other than that, we don't know much.

Pharnacia kirbyi

These huge phasmids come from Borneo, where they are the largest insects. They live exclusively in the trees, never coming to the ground.

Chapter 4) Buying stick insects

You've decided on what type of stick insect you want. You've worked out the space and feeding requirements. Now you just need to get hold of them. This is, surprisingly, much easier than most people expect, even with very exotic and unusual types, as long as you are willing to wait or hatch yourself.

What?

You need to know what age of stick insect you're going to buy, not just the species. Depending on your requirements and resources you could be best suited to getting eggs/ova, nymphs (hatched out babies) or adults. They each have their advantages and disadvantages.

Eggs/ova

If you're feeling patient, this is a great option for a tight budget. You can often buy 10 eggs for the same price as you'd pay for a single adult. In addition, if you are distance buying (online) the postage is a lot less, as they can be sent in plastic medical phials as a large letter, rather than in a larger box as a package.
They are also a great way of getting some of the rarer types of stick insect, as some collectors of more hard to get stick insects will sell off any excess eggs so that they are not overrun, but won't part with nymphs or adults. This is also a good way to

learn about lifecycles if you are getting stick insects as an educational tool.

There are a few problems with buying eggs, though. The main one is the time they take to hatch. You need to remember to keep them damp, but not wet, and warm, for up to 7 months. This can be a real pain, especially if children are waiting for something to happen. They can hatch in only a few months, or if you have a friendly breeder they might sell you some that only have another month to wait. Even so, it's easy to forget about them. If you do remember to keep them at the right conditions and you're patient enough, you still might not have a high hatch rate. With the right conditions you can expect about 50% to hatch.

Nymphs

Nymphs are newly hatched insects. Stick insect nymphs are a great place to start. You can watch them grow and develop, from little tiny crawling things into strong, majestic adults. They grow quite quickly and they change dramatically. They are usually quite dull and plain when they are very young. But as they grow and change the colours that they'll have as an adult begin to show, and (in winged species) the wings begin to develop.

The thing with getting nymphs is that they are very delicate and often too small to be handled right away. In addition, they aren't as interesting to look at as adults. There will also be a few months before they are at their best. And there will be a long wait for any eggs.

Adults

Adult stick insects are in their prime. They are interesting to watch, much easier to see and easy to care for. They will start laying eggs as soon as they are adult and mated, although some will reproduce through parthenogenesis. Adult stick insects make the most impressive display animal.

The down side here is that you don't get to watch them grow and change.

Where?

The next thing you need to decide is where you are going to get your stick insects from. There are lots of outlets for the different stick insects you might want. Where you choose to purchase your phasmids from will depend on your choice of species and other varying requirements. Each source has its pros and cons.

a) Bug fairs

Bug fairs are fantastic places to get live insects from. They are full of knowledgeable stallholders who will be able to advise you further. You can get everything you need in one place. You can also inspect them before you take them home. Live insects should be lively and bright.

The problem with bug fairs is that there is no way of knowing what there will be there. If you have your heart set on a specific species, you might find that no one at the fair has brought any with them.

b) Pet shops

A pet shop is a great place to get insects from, having all the same positives as bug fairs – good advice, a face-to-face sale, you get to see them before you buy them – and more. As well as the same great incentives as bug fairs, you have more choice. While there may not be a great range of stick insects in store, many pet shops that stock stick insects will also be able to order in different species from their supplier.

The problem with pet shops is that they will have to charge you more as they have permanent overheads. They also tend to keep their stock together, with little or no quarantine period.

c) Online – auctions or shops

Online retailers of insects tend to be real enthusiasts and breeders. This means that everything they have will be a result of a treasured pet/collection piece. These people understand that the quality and health of the animals is paramount and are more likely to sell only healthy, strong animals. There is also a lot more choice out there, as you are not restricted to what is available locally. There is a huge variety out there. Because online auction sites let you see the feedback of other customers, you can check to make sure their feedback is good. There will be comments about packaging of live insects and the health of them too. You will also have much more recourse if anything goes wrong – sellers on auction sites are terrified of bad feedback and very helpful, and if the insects don't arrive then it is easy for you to get your money back. As well as the huge variety available, there is a range of ages of insect available too. Online shops are also very good places to get stick insects and eggs/ova from as they will often be private breeders selling off healthy animals.

The downside here is the postage cost. The cost of posting live insects is much higher than posting eggs/ova because of the size of the package involved. If you're buying online you really do get an economy of scale. If you buy a number of insects from the same breeder then you can make real savings in postage. The other problem with distance buying is that you can't see the insects before they arrive, but most sellers have a good returns policy.

d) Online – forums

The best bit about joining a forum for a specialised pet like stick insects is the sense of community and support it provides. One of the great perks of this is, when your stick insects are grown up and healthy and laying little eggs of their own, you can use them as a sort of currency with other owners on the forums. For example, my first Phaenopharos Khaoyaiensis came from 15 eggs that I'd swapped for 50 Indian stick insect eggs. There are also the same advantages as buying at online stores and auction sites – good range, good health good service.

Not only are the positives the same as online shops and auctions, the negatives are the same –postage costs can be high for nymphs and adults and you can't see them before you buy them.

Chapter 5) Handling

Stick insects are pets. This means lots of things, but most of all it means they'll need to be handled, at least when it's cleaning out time, and often more than that.

The most important thing to remember when handling any animal is that we don't really know where they've been. You should always wash your hands after handling your stick insects. They might have sprayed noxious chemicals onto your hands that could hurt your eyes or numb your mouth. They might also have pee and poop on their feet.

a) Handling adults

All varieties of stick insect will let you handle them and generally like this as long as you are not too rough. Wings, legs and antennae break easily so the utmost care is required when handling them, and it is also a good idea to keep them away from cats or any other pets that you might have.

They should especially be kept away from any rodents you own. Mice and rats and hamsters will happily gobble up stick insects. As will terrapins, (as I found out the hard way!) if the stick insects escape and get into their tank.

Flying stick insects should be let out in a small room occasionally to have a good soar about. A bathroom with the toilet lid down and the plugs in is a good place to do this, as it's easy to find them again afterwards.

Some of the larger species such as the Giant Malaysian may also give the handler a nip on the hand if they are not used to handling, but this is not painful and is quite uncommon.

If you are worried about hurting your stick insects, you can pick them up by touching their back feet, gently, until they lift them off whatever surface they're living on. Then you can put your hand underneath the stick insect and move your hand to the next set of legs. Then when these feet let go, put your hand under them, and so on until you've picked them up. This is also a good way to put the down again afterwards.

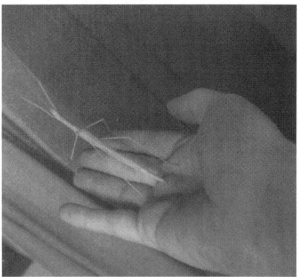

You can also use their obsessive compulsion to be on the top of everything to your advantage to pick them up. When a stick insect is awake at the top of their food plant, simply hold your fingers over the top of it. You may need to stimulate them to move by gently brushing their feet. Then they should just climb onto your hand.

Because of their delicate feet and bodies, you need to be careful about hurting them. Their feet have 2 little hooks on the ends to hold on to their environment. They should never be simply picked up or grabbed. When they are on your hands or clothing, you have to be very careful taking them off, as they can damage their feet when they grip their hooks into you. While it won't hurt you, it can pull their little hooks and feet off.

b) Handling nymphs

Very little nymphs shouldn't be picked up. They are so small and delicate that the slightest pressure could damage or even kill them. You should move them on food plants or with the bristles of fine paintbrushes.

c) Handling eggs

When you are handling the eggs, too, you need to be very careful. You should pick them up with soft tipped tweezers, or with a damp paintbrush, as many stick insect eggs will crush easily. If your stick insect has laid eggs through leaves or attached to a surface, however, it is generally considered best not to move them.

d) Posting live stick insects

If you ever have to send live stick insects through the post you need to be very careful of how you package them.

You will need:
Plastic container (take away box is ideal)
Paper towel
3 elastic bands
A sharp knife or drill
Some food plants
A padded envelope

What you need to do first is make a series of holes in the box, in the lid for breathing and 2 at each end of the box. Lay the paper towel on the bottom of the box, folded up and damp. Poke 2 sprigs of the food plants through, so that they are held in place by the holes at either end of the box. Then wrap some damp paper towel around the ends of the food plant that are sticking out of the box, to keep the food plant fresh for the journey.

Next use one of the elastic bands on each end to anchor the food plants to each other, so that they don't move about in transit. It is very important that the food plants don't move about inside the box. Their relative stability is what will keep the stick insects safe. Then put your stick insects in the box and pop the lid on. With the last elastic band, secure the lid in place.

DO NOT TAPE THE LID ON as this can make it difficult to remove the stick insects, and if the recipient can't get all the tape off the sides of the box you could end up with little sticks loosing legs if their feet get stuck.

Finally, put the whole thing in a padded envelope labelled fragile and send by first class or next day delivery. Try not to post on Fridays to avoid them being left in the cold sorting office over the weekend, and try not to post in the winter.

e) Posting eggs

Posting eggs is far simpler and cheaper. A simple plastic phial will keep the eggs safe in transit. You can buy these on eBay or at pharmaceutical websites for pennies. Simply place a piece of damp –not wet – paper towel or cotton wool in the bottom of the phial. From there, you can put as many eggs as you're sending into the phial, though don't overfill or 'squash' the eggs in, as they can be crushed. The eggs can be sent in this manner by any service you like.

DO NOT POST INSECTS OR INSECT EGGS INTERNATIONALLY as there are often laws about this. Many countries take their bio security very seriously, especially island nations such as Australia and New Zeeland.

Chapter 6) Housing

There are all sorts of stick insect enclosures. I will refer to them as cages, even though some of them are clearly tanks, because there should always be at least one wall that is some sort of mesh. You can buy stick insect cages that are specifically designed for your specific type of stick, but these tend to be more expensive than necessary, and most stick insect cages can be adapted with the clever use of card to reduce airflow.

If you have decided to hatch eggs yourself, you can do this in a plastic takeaway box. You should cut air holes in the lid, before you put the eggs in, and lay a piece of paper towel on the bottom.

As the nymphs grow, they will need a larger cage, but nowhere too big, so that they will easily be able to find and eat food. You can put them in with adults when they are a couple of weeks old.

a) Bought cages

As with many things in life, you can buy ready-made cages for stick insects that are very good and not too expensive, or you can make your own. There is a growing array of professionally made cages that are suitable for stick insects. They are often designed for other creatures, such as butterflies.

Pop ups

The most popular, though in my view least attractive, is the pop up stick insect cage. These are 6 squarish loops of wire making a cubiod, covered in fine netting. There is a zip opening at the side for access. There are a number of different types of these available, including the Magicage, at about £9 or $15, which is usually sold for butterflies, the Gribblybugs large net cage, which are much taller and are about £20 or $33 and the Bugzarre pop up at £10 or $17. The largest available pop up is 5foot tall and will set you back £80, or $130.

These can also be adapted from the pop up laundry baskets that you can get in supermarkets for about £4 or $7.

Vivariums

Vivariums, or vivs as they are usually called when you're buying them second hand in forums, are a much more attractive option, though they can be very expensive new, there are some very nice ones that you can get for under £50 or about $80. Hailea do a very nice reptile cage that is flat pack so you don't even need to collect it. They are black hexagonal plastic frames with black netting. These are also more stable than the pop ups.

You can make a viv yourself out of wooden frames and netting. There are loads of videos of how to do this online, but once you factor in parts and labour, this probably isn't the sort of cage you'd make yourself.

Vented plastic cage

The vented plastic cage is only suitable for certain types of stick insect, as it doesn't offer as much ventilation as many of them need. Bugzarre do a solo jar, a small plastic container with a tip vent for £7 or $12. This cage looks like a large sweet jar and works well for smaller stick insects and juveniles. They also do a Tall Ultra Vent option, which has 4 vents on 2 sides and is more suited to medium stick insects. This is a nice, secure house but isn't very clear to see through at your insects. It normally costs £18 or $30.

b) Homemade cages

You can make a really nice cage for stick insects that will suit your requirements exactly. Many collectors and breeders use homemade cages.

Homemade vented plastic cage

These can be easily made for suitable, secure closing plastic containers. You can use ones that you already have, or buy them from supermarkets or online for a couple of quid. Then you need a hole saw/a neighbour with a hole saw that is the same size as a curtain eyelet. You can get curtain eyelets at DIY stores. A pack of 10 will be about £4 or $7. Then you place one half of the eyelet inside the hole with the tube/middle part sticking through, place a piece of fabric over the hole and press the outside of the eyelet over the fabric and the plastic, locking it all together to make a vent. Or you can buy a ready made vent and use that.

It's useful to make these yourself if you need a lot. If you were making 10 of these, they would cost about £5 or $8 each to make.

Custom vivs

Most collectors and hobbyists who've been doing this a long time will make their own, custom vivs to the spec they need and using materials available to them. This is where your imagination can run wild and you can really get some good ideas from online. I personally have 4 custom vivs.

One made from a broken, clear under bed storage box. This is a real beauty. The bottom smashed off in an incident. I then cut the bottom out clean and stuck some leftover voile mesh to the bottom. Then I cut out the middle of the lid and covered it in the same stuff. Turned on it's end, this makes a great home for my

Parapachymorpha zomproi and Extatosoma tiaratuma, as they need lots of ventilation.

I have a small-vented baby viv for the hatchlings. I made this from an empty plastic sweet jar; I think it used to contain Roses. I drilled a large hole in the lid and stuck some voile over the hole. This is difficult to clean out and is only really used for babies.

For the vicious jungle nymphs, the Heteropteryx dilatata, who don't need much ventilation, I use an old fish tank. As it wasn't watertight any more it was given away for free! I keep this on its side, tall and slim, with a net curtain held over the opening with an elastic band.

The Sipyloidea sipylus, sweet pink winged stick insects, which live with the pretty Achrioptera Punctipes Punctipes, have the biggest cage of all. It is about 4 foot tall and is made from old wood and a plastic cold frame. A cold frame is a frame that sits on the ground with the faces having plastic or glass in them and one side being open. The one I used had an opening lid. I turned this on its side and covered the bottom in voile.

A pain in the neck it may be, but different types if stick insects need different types of housing. Not only do larger ones and flying ones need more room, but also some smaller and more delicate ones can't be kept in mixed cages for their own safety. Also, some need warmer temperatures than others. Some stick insects need a lot of breeze or draft, others need very little.

Whatever the specifics of the stick insect breeds you have chosen, one thing is for certain- as much space as you can afford to give them is usually best. They need the height of their cage to be at least 3 times their length. This will allow them room to shed their skin safely. They need the footprint of their cage to be at least 2.5 times their length squared, so that they can turn around comfortably. If you have 2 or more (and you really should because they are social animals and there isn't any more work involved in keeping 10 than there is in keeping 1) then the footprint should be at least twice this.

All phasmids come from tropical environments. Because of this, they all have specific humidity requirements. The instructions that follow will tell you how to keep them humid enough. The instruction to "spray" the cage means that you should have a spray bottle just for them. If your spray bottle is kept for only this use, there is no danger of it ever containing anything that could harm the stick insects.

When you spray them, you should spray one squirt of water into the cage, avoiding any phasmids or eggs. This will make the air damp enough. By keeping a paper towel on the base of the cage, you can monitor the humidity of the enclosure. If you make sure the paper is never completely dry, then you'll know the air isn't too dry for your delicate sticks.

You should never allow any water to pool on the floor of the cage, though, as this will encourage mould and could drown the small nymphs, or even adult stick insects as they aren't clever.

Some stick insects can live together happily, based on their housing needs and their temperament. Others really need to be kept away from other types of stick insect as they can be aggressive and damage the smaller ones.

c) Species specific housing

Achrioptera

The Achrioptera need large, airy cages. They need room to hang and room to fly safely. Cramped conditions and too many food plants can obstruct flight and damage wings. They need airflow to keep them clean and to help them breathe, so at least 2 sides should be mesh. The ideal cage for Achrioptera would be a pop up cage of some sort, although these cages aren't very pretty, and they will do well with a more attractive cage as long as there is enough ventilation. They need a lot of humidity, too, and a daily spraying, or twice-daily if the air is very dry, is required to allow for shedding and growth. You can tell if they need spraying again by looking at the paper towel on the base. If it is ever dry, they should be sprayed again.

Acrophylla Wuflfingi

The sleek Acrophylla Wuflfingi needs room for flying and so shouldn't be kept anywhere small. They don't need a lot of humidity, being Australian, but they can't be allowed to dry out. They can be kept moist enough by keeping a damp paper towel or cloth on the base and keeping it damp. The evaporated water will be enough to keep them moist. They don't need much ventilation, so a vented plastic cage will provide enough airflow. A small heat mat will be appreciated.

Diapherodes Gigantea

Big and bulky, Diapherodes Gigantea need a large cage with good ventilation and room for the males to fly without hurting their wings. A large pop up would be ideal for them, as the sides are soft and easy to climb, and they provide lots of airflow. They can live happily at room temperature if it's warmish. You should spray them every other day to keep humidity up, and have a damp paper towel on the floor.

Parapachymorpha zomproi

Thin and delicate, the Parapachymorpha zomproi don't need a huge enclosure, as they aren't very big and don't fly. They need good ventilation and fairly humid conditions – but don't need spraying, because they will be kept warm with a small heat mat and a damp paper towel on the base will stop the air from drying out.

Extatosoma Tiaratum

Grumpy, aggressive and fat, Extatosoma Tiaratum should be kept on their own, in a species-specific cage. They need room to bumble about and height to climb, as, despite their weight, they like to climb. As an Australian species, Extatosoma Tiaratum should be kept warm. A heat mat will be appreciated. They can stand quite still air, and a vented plastic cage will do nicely.

They also do well in an upturned glass tank with a net screen over the open side.

Phaenopharos Khaoyaiensis

The Phaenopharos Khaoyaiensis like moderate temperatures, so they would do well at room temperature. They want a mesh cage of 50-80cm of height if they can have it. They need a nice lot of room. The Phaenopharos Khaoyaiensis should be kept humid and they need to be sprayed regularly, at least once a day.

Neophasma subapterum

This is a small species that doesn't like big open spaces. It's good to keep some couples in a cage from 30 cm cubed. A fauna box, a vented plastic cage, is perfect. They like to hide, so some hiding places are recommended, like tree bark and fallen leaves. If there is a lot of vegetation in the cage, they will be much happier. It may sound odd, but the more hiding spaces they have, the less they will hide.

Ramulus nematodes Blue

They need to be kept warm and humid, spraying every day, but there should be no puddles of water on the base, and you should keep a close eye out for mould. The cage doesn't need too much ventilation. A glass tank with a net screen over the open side will keep them humid enough and allow them enough ventilation. They will appreciate a heat mat or a radiator.

They shouldn't be kept with any of the big, heavy species, as they are very delicate, but they can be kept with other fine phasmids.

Peruphasma schultei

While they aren't aggressive, as such, the Peruphasma schultei are very robust, and shouldn't be kept with delicate species, as they could damage them accidentally if they climb on them. They like little humidity, being kept on a damp paper towel should suffice. They should be kept warm and relatively still, needing only a little ventilation. They also need to be able to hide, leaves are best. You have to be careful when getting rid of the dead leaves.

Neohiasea maerens.

The Neohiasea maerens should really be sprayed regularly, though they aren't too bothered by being a little dry, and need a tall cage with a light substrate on the ground in a tray. You have to be very careful of mould with damp, but good ventilation will help keep the mould down. They need lots of ventilation and a pop up mesh cage would be the best type of enclosure.

Asceles

They should be kept in a large, tall cage, with good ventilation; a mesh pop up cage will be the best for them. They need lots of humidity and regular spraying. They don't need any substrate, but like a damp paper towel. Asceles are happy at room temperature.

Heteropteryx dilatata

The Heteropteryx dilatata are far too aggressive to be kept with anyone else. They need enough room to get away from each other but they don't need flying room. The temperature can vary between 20 ° C and 30 ° C. Room temperature is fine for this species, but growth can be delayed if kept at low temperatures. This species needs high air humidity. Spray at least five times a week to allow the insects to drink from the droplets and to keep the humidity up. Ventilation is very important, without enough of it, *Heteroperyx dilatata* will get problems with mould and bacteria. A larger cage is always better and is also necessary if you keep multiple individuals. At the bottom of the enclosure you need to place a layer of moist soil, sand or potting earth. The female lays her eggs in the soil with her ovipositor.

Longhodes Philippinicus

They do not require any fancy equipment at all. They like little humidity, being kept on a damp paper towel should suffice. They should be kept warm and relatively still, needing only a little ventilation. They also need to be able to hide, leaves are best. You have to be careful when getting rid of the dead leaves.

Xenophasmina

The Xenophasmina loves a humid environment, with spraying at least once a day – though not so much as to leave puddles. They like a substrate to hide on and thin twigs to hang on. They need

52

good ventilation, with preferably 2 or more sides of the cage providing a draft. This is why they need to be sprayed so often. They do well at room temperature and don't need to be heated, as long as it's not a particularly cold room.

Mearnsiana Bullosa

Because of their mountain origins, they are used to a light breeze. They need good ventilation and thrive at room temperature. They need humidity, but not too much – a damp paper towel will keep them humid enough, but you need to make sure it doesn't dry out. A large pop up would be ideal for them, as the sides are soft and easy to climb, and they provide lots of airflow. They can live happily at room temperature if it's warmish. You should spray them every other day to keep humidity up, and have a damp paper towel on the floor.

Lopaphus Magnificus

The Lopaphus Magnificus can live in most types of cages, as they aren't too fussy. They shouldn't be kept too dry, though. They need to be kept warm, but not much warmer than room temperature of 23C. They can be kept by a warm window in the summer and by the radiator in winter. They can be kept with other species that have the same requirements.

Cranidium Gibbosum

If you plan to breed these guys then you should keep them in a net type cage, as they fling their eggs very hard and can break them on glass. They can grow to a good size so will need quite a bit of room for moulting etc. The Cranidium Gibbosum needs to be kept quite humid, so a spray every other day to every day in dry conditions is a good idea. When they are very young they should be sprayed daily. They live very happily at room temperature.

These phasmids, because of their leaf like bodies, should not be kept in mixed cages as they can get nibbled on. Because of their slight cannibal tendencies, they shouldn't be kept in too crowded conditions either.

Eurycantha Calcarata

They need more flat space than other phasmids. They do well at room temperature. This species has to be kept moist. We recommend spraying the enclosure about 4 times a week. Make sure there is a lot of potting earth or humus at the bottom of the terrarium. Keep this moist, but do not allow mould to develop.

This species needs a thick layer of moist earth, sand, vermiculite or potting ground at the bottom of the terrarium. The females lay their eggs in the ground. You also need to offer the animals a place to hide under, like a broken flower pot, a shallow wooden box or a piece of rock that is a bit lifted from the ground. They will crawl under anything that is dark and a bit moist. This species does need branches to hang from when moulting, so be sure to supply these too!

Tirachoidea Jianfenglingensis

Because of their size, the Tirachoidea Jianfenglingensis needs a lot of room to move about and moult. Also, due to the fact that the males can fly, they do need room to stretch their wings where they won't be damaged.

They do well at room temperature and they need a good level of humidity. A spray every other day should do it, making sure that there are no puddles left. They should have a paper towel on the floor to catch any eggs, as they will be thrown quite heavily to the ground.

Pharnacia kirbyi

Large and long, the Pharnacia kirbyi need a big cage to move about and moult safely. Because they grow to up to 20 inches long, they need a cage of at least 60 inches, preferably more. One collector I know keeps his in a converted wardrobe, with the back taken out and replaced with aluminium mesh, and the panels in the doors have been replaced too. They need warm, humid conditions with moderate ventilation. Keep them next to a radiator and spray twice daily. Due to their size, they can't be kept with other phasmids, because, while they aren't aggressive, they can accidentally damage others.

Chapter 7) Feeding

While it is best to try and feed your stick insects on as varied a diet as you can, they will often only eat certain types of plants. A lot of them also eat plants that are not available everywhere. The suggestions for feeding are based on plants that are readily available in most locations. Collect food plants from areas that have not been sprayed with insecticides and avoid plants that are next to busy roads.

The important thing to remember when feeding your stick insects is that they aren't very clever. Just look at the size of them – there isn't much room for a brain in their tiny heads. You need to be aware, all the time, that delicate little morons are going to be bumbling about in the cage, so you have to be careful of their safety.

The food plants, if cut from the live plants, need to be put into water. This is where the problem with the stick insects not being too bright comes in. You can't just put the cut plants into a jar of water. If you do this, then the stick insects will drown in the water.

You can put cotton wool or paper towels over the water to stop them falling in. This will be enough to protect them. You can also use old jam jars that have plastic lids. If you cut holes in these for the food plants to fit in, the lids will help to keep the stick insects from drowning.

Another way to deal with this problem is to plant the food. Plant pots of clean earth and little plants in them will mean that you don't have to replace the food too often. This will also provide somewhere for eggs to be laid. If you bake the soil before you use it, then there won't be any pathogens or predators that can harm your phasmids.

Another problem the phasmids have in captivity is the roof. Stick insects have a real urge to get to the roof of their cage. In the wild they hang from the highest leaves for safety. In captivity, however, they hang from the ceiling.

The problem that this causes them is rather a stupid one. It is something quite funny, or it would be. Stick insects will often starve before they go down to the bottom to find food. They literally need to walk into food to know that it's there.

What this means, in practical terms, is that you have to make sure that their food plants reach the top of the cage, bending on the top is best.

In the winter, you might find that the food plants die back. What, then, can you feed your stick insects?

Most stick insects will eat evergreen plants, as well as the deciduous ones that they prefer. This means that in the winter you may be able to feed them ivy, or privet. If they aren't too fond of these types of food plant, there is something you can do.

You can dry the food plants through the summer. By making sure you always collect twice as much as you need and drying half, you can store enough food for the winter. You will have to soak the dried food plants before you feed them to your phasmids, so that they can eat them. The dry crunchy leaves will be too hard.

Achrioptera

The stick insects in the Achrioptera line such as Achrioptera punctipes cliquennoisi, Achrioptera Fallax and Achrioptera Punctipes Punctipes, will generally eat the same food.

It still isn't known what these eat in the wild, but in captivity they thrive on bramble, raspberry, salal, and oak, which are very common in the UK and the USA. They also like guava, rose apple and eucalyptus. You should offer as many different types of food as possible, as a varied diet provides different levels of nutrients.

Acrophylla Wuflfingi

The Acrophylla Wuflfingi will need a lot to eat – they grow quite big and do eat for their size. They'll happily eat Bramble, Oak, Raspberry, Rose, and Red/ Yellow Salmon Berry. They will also eat eucalyptus if you have any growing near you. You should offer as many different types of food as possible, as a varied diet provides different levels of nutrients.

Diapherodes Gigantea

The stick insects in the Diapherodes group will all live happily on bramble, raspberry, salal, dog rose and beech, which are easily come by in the UK and USA. They like Acacia muricata (spineless wattle), Persea Americana (avocado) and Ocotea coriacea (lancewood) if you have any growing near you – mine eat a couple of avocado plants that I grew from the stones of the fruit. They will also take cherry laurel, though only as a supplementary plant, as they can live on just this. You should offer as many different types of food as possible, as a varied diet provides different levels of nutrients.

Borneo Giant Thorny Stick Insects

The heavy, veracious Borneo giant thorny stick insect is a ravenous creature, feeding heavily on bramble, oak and ivy. They need to be fed often, as they are really hungry guys, with bodies that aren't very efficient. You should offer as many different types of food as possible, as a varied diet provides different levels of nutrients.

Parapachymorpha zomproi

The Parapachymorpha zomproi are another robust stick insect that eats well. They eat bramble, hawthorn and rose. Mine will nibble a bit of ivy, but they don't go mad for it. It isn't known what else they eat, but it won't harm to try them on other plants. You should offer as many different types of food as possible, as a varied diet provides different levels of nutrients.

Extatosoma Tiaratum

The big, aggressive Extaosoma Tiaratum eats well. They will eat a wide range of things, from bramble, eucalyptus, photinia, hawthorn, raspberry, oak, rose, and pyrocantha and you can try ivy. You should offer as many different types of food as possible, as a varied diet provides different levels of nutrients.

Phaenopharos Khaoyaiensis

Phaenopharos Khaoyaiensis eat much more delicately than a lot of other phasmids. They'll nibble happily on bramble, hawthorn, hypericum, and raspberry. They have also been known to eat privet. As with all stick insects, you should offer as many different types of food as possible, as a varied diet provides different levels of nutrients.

Neophasma subapterum

The fat bodied Neophasma subapterum will happily eat privet and honeysuckle. If there is any in your area, they will also gobble up plantain, lilac and osmanthus. They need to have access to a lot of food. Their bodies are heavy and they need a lot of energy to move about. You should offer as many different types of food as possible, as a varied diet provides different levels of nutrients.

Ramulus nematodes Blue

The beautiful and delicate Ramulus nematodes Blue eats bramble, rose and raspberry. They also thrive on oak leaves. They need the food to reach to the top of their enclosures more than most, as they will rarely come down from the roof. You should offer as many different types of food as possible, as a varied diet provides different levels of nutrients.

Peruphasma schultei

The robust black beauty will eat privet and honeysuckle. The newly hatched nymphs will need the edges of the leaves nipping off, as they are too hard for them to eat. You should offer both privet and honeysuckle if you can, as a varied diet provides different levels of nutrients.

Neohiasea maerens

The Neohiasea maerens should be fed older bramble, not new leaves, ivy and oak. They need their food plants to be kept damp, but not so wet as to drip. The plants should be kept tall and fresh. To keep the nutrients varied, you should offer as many different types of food plants as you can find.

Asceles

These are very picky eaters, they like Juglans regia, (walnut) leaves and Hypericum. They prefer walnut but Hypericum is commonly kept in gardens and is easier to get hold of.

Heteropteryx dilatata

The Heteropteryx dilatata are very good eaters. Their food plants grow wild in most locations. They will eat bramble, raspberry, ivy and oak. They will also eat privet.

Longhodes Philippinicus

The Longhodes Philippinicus will eat privet and eucalyptus. There isn't a massive amount of information about what these beauties eat, but if they are in a mixed enclosure they may nibble other things too. If you see this, take note and see if they eat it again. This is information that other owners would appreciate you sharing on forums.

Xenophasmina

The Xenophasmina eats bramble, raspberry, beach, oak and salal. All of these grow wild and should be fairly easy to get hold of. You should give as many different types of food as you can to keep the variation of nutrients.

Mearnsiana Bullosa

The chunky Mearnsiana Bullosa is really not that fussy. They like bramble and oak and raspberry if they can get it.

Lopaphus Magnificus

The lovely Lopaphus Magnificus will eat Bramble, Hypericum and oak Oak. Some will nibble on ivy, though not all of them.

Cranidium Gibbosum

The leafy Cranidium Gibbosum likes Salal, Buche, oak and raspberry. They also love bramble. There are other members of the bramble family that they eat too, try them with a few things and see what they go for.

This species eats a lot. They are a very hungry lot and if they don't get enough food they have been known to turn on each other.

Eurycantha Calcarata

The Eurycantha Calcarata will eat Bramble, raspberry, ivy, fire thorn, chestnut, hazel and rose and oak. They like to eat all sorts of other things that also make nice houseplants, such as umbrella plants and rubber plants. As they are ground dwelling creatures, they would also eat windfall, and do well on the odd slice of apple.

Tirachoidea Jianfenglingensis

The huge Tirachoidea Jianfenglingensis eats oak, bramble, rose, salal and hazel. They will also eat eucalyptus if provided.

Pharnacia kirbyi

Long, thin and delicate, the Pharnacia kirbyi, despite being the longest stick insect ever recorded, eats surprisingly few species of plant. They eat only oak and guava. If, for whatever reason, you decide to keep Pharnacia kirbyi, you need to feed them both of these, to make sure there is enough variation in their food.

a) Collecting food plants

You should always know where the food plants you feed to your stick insects comes from. You need to make sure that it is free of pesticides and hasn't grown too close to main roads. You also need to make sure that it doesn't bring in any other insects. A spider in the cage will happily eat up any small nymphs it can find.

b) Grow your own

One of the ways to make sure your stick insects always have fresh food plant is to grow your own. It is simple enough to propagate all of their food plant one way or another, ether from seed or from cuttings.

Privet

If you don't have your own privet hedge and the neighbors object to you trimming theirs, you can grow privet in a pot in the cage from cuttings. Growing privet from cutting is very easy.

You will need:
clean compost or coir
a plant pot
plant cutting

Take a few cuttings so that you have a few options, or lots of plants to feed your stick insects. You simply push the cuttings into the earth in the pot. Privet doesn't need any rooting compound in order to root, but you can use it if you like. Alternatively, you can use cuttings that have rooted from the pot of water. My Lonchodes Philippinicus nymphs love theirs, and it makes an attractive display.

Rose

The easiest way to propagate a rose plant for your stick insects cage is from a cutting.

You will need:
Sand
Plant pot
Jar
Rooting hormone / aspirin
Soil
Gardening gloves

Fill the plant pot with sand. Poke a hole in the sand with your finger for the cutting.

Wear gardening gloves to protect your hands from thorns. Make several small cuts along the stem of your cutting. Keep the gloves on while you cover all the fresh cuts with the growth hormone powder.

Place the cutting into the hole. Immediately place the cutting into the hole you prepared with the knitting needle.

If you are propagating from a rose stem, push the stem all the way into the hole until the bottom of the flower head touches the surface of the sand.

If you are propagating a cutting with leaves, push the stem down far enough that at least five of the leaves are not in the ground. It will look like a tiny plant.

House the cutting. Place the jar over the cutting and water. In approximately nine months, the cutting will have taken root and will be a new baby rose bush for your garden.

If you are propagating during the summer, it's important to water the cutting regularly, as you would a normal rose bush. However, if you are propagating in the fall, simply leave it alone until spring and remove the jar when you see new growth and there is no more threat of frost.

Once your rose trees have rooted, you can put them in your stick insect cage. Its a good idea to do a dozen or so cuttings so that you can choose the best for your sticks.

Avocados

The next time you eat an avocado or use one in a recipe, save the stone or pit. Planting your own avocado tree is fun and easy. It is perfect for all ages – for the garden, for indoors and it also makes a great project for class or at home.

Wash the avocado pit gently to remove all of the flesh. Be careful not to remove the seed cover which is light brown in color.

Holding the pit "narrow" (pointed) side up, stick four toothpicks into the middle section at even intervals, to a depth of about 5 mm.

Add some water to a small, slender container (preferably glass) until it reaches the very top rim. Your container's opening should be wide enough to easily accommodate the full width of the avocado pit. However, make sure that it is not too wide.

Set your avocado pit (with inserted toothpicks) on the top rim of the container. The toothpicks should sit on the rim of the container, leaving the pit only half-submerged in the water. Make sure the pointed end is up and the rounded end is in the water, otherwise your avocado will not grow.

Set the avocado-topped container in a temperate, undisturbed place – near a window or any other well-lit area in order to begin rooting and the growth process.

Change the water every 1-2 days. Do this to ensure that contaminants (i.e. mold, bacteria, fermentation, etc.) do not hinder the avocado's sprouting process. Ensure that the base of the avocado always remains moist and submerged in water.

Wait patiently since avocado takes several weeks to start growing its roots. Over the next 2-3 weeks, the avocado's brown outer layer will begin to dry out and wrinkle, eventually sloughing off. Soon after, the pit should begin to split open at the top and bottom. After 3-4 weeks, a tap root should begin to emerge at the base of the pit.

Continue to water the plant accordingly. Take care not to disturb or injure the tap root. Continue to allow the avocado pit time to establish its roots. Soon, the avocado will sprout at the top, releasing an unfolding leaf-bud that will open and begin to grow a shoot bearing leaves.

Plant the baby tree. When the roots are substantial and the stem top has had a chance to re-grow leaves (after at least one pruning), your baby avocado tree is ready to be planted in soil. Remove the sprouted pit from the water container, and gently remove each of the toothpicks.

Use a 20-25 cm terracotta pot filled with enriched soil to 2 cm below the top. A 50/50 blend of topsoil and coir (coconut fibre) works best. Smooth and slightly pack the soil, adding more soil as needed. Once the soil is prepared, dig a narrow hole deep enough to accommodate your avocado's roots and pit.

Carefully bury the avocado pit in the soil such that the top-half of the pit shows above the surface of the soil. This ensures that the base of the seedling trunk doesn't rot under the soil. Pack the soil lightly around the pit.

Water your plant daily or enough to keep the soil moist. Avoid over-watering to the point that the soil becomes muddy. If the leaves turn brown at the tips, the tree needs more water. If the leaves turn yellow, the tree is getting too much water and needs to be permitted to dry out for a day or two.

Continue to tend to your avocado plant regularly, and in a few years you will have an attractive and low-maintenance tree. Your family and friends will be impressed to know that from an avocado pit, salvaged from your guacamole recipe, you have cultivated and grown your very own avocado tree. Alternatively, plant the pit in a pot during the warmer months and wait for 3-4 months for the plant to sprout.

Bramble, raspberry and blackberry

You want to root brambles. Just cut a bit off and shove it in a hole, or take a branch and layer it, (peg it down onto the soil with a large staple or bent wire), or poke an end of a branch in a hole or a pot, whilst still attached to the parent. In fact you could shake a bit of bramble at the soil and it would take root. Don't worry about killing the cutting, YOU WON'T. Brambles have a very strong desire to take over the world.

Oak

During October and November, you need to go out and collect the acorns you are going to grow. Try to collect from the healthiest trees you see, so that yours will grow strong. Also try to collect from mature trees in groups, not isolated individuals.

You will then also need to consider what sort of container to grow them in. You can use a plant pot, but why not try using a large yoghurt pot or cut the bottom off an empty plastic bottle?

Soak the acorns overnight in warm water. Then carefully peel off the outer shell. Try not to damage the inner seed (called the kernel), as this is the part of the nut that will grow into a tree.

Cut some holes in the base of your pot and put some stones at the bottom to help with drainage. Then put in some soil or peat free compost so that the pot is about two-thirds full. Finally, stand the pot on a saucer.

Place three acorns in your pot (a single acorn may not survive) and cover with a layer of soil. Cover your pot with a plastic bag and put it in a sunny place on the windowsill.

As soon as you see the seedlings appear (this is called germination) remove the bag. Make sure you water the seedlings once or twice a week and keep the soil moist.

When the seedlings grow to a height of approximately 75mm, choose the seedling that looks the strongest as this has the greatest chance of survival. Remove the other two seedlings, which could then be replanted into new pots. The remaining seedling now has more room to grow.

During October and November, you need to go out and collect the acorns you are going to grow. Try to collect from the healthiest trees you see, so that yours will grow strong. Also try to collect from mature trees in groups, not isolated individuals.

Eucalyptus

Hardy Eucalyptus seeds always benefit from a cold period at 3 - 5 deg C, usually 2 months in the refridgerator. We tend to store our seeds in the refridgerator so this is not always necessary when you receive them (we will indicate if you need to cold treat them).

Eucalyptus seedlings hate their roots being disturbed at any time during their growth. Therefore, we tend to choose a pot or tray that is deep enough to allow the tap root to grow unhindered until it is ready for potting on. A standard 2 - 3 inch deep seed tray is fine, otherwise try some deeper pots.

Fill your chosen tray or pot with a good general purpose compost, water it well and leave it to drain. Place the tray or pot in a propagator for 24hrs bringing it up to the required germination temperature (15 - 20 deg C). If you don't have a propagator simply cover the top of your pot with a clear plastic bag held in place with an elastic band. (If you cant achieve this temperature, dont worry, your seeds will still germinate but may take a while longer).

Sprinkle the fine seeds thinly onto the surface of your prewarmed compost and place them back into your chosen propagator. Keep a weekly eye on your seeds. Never allow them to dry out as they will die. If you need to, simply mist the surface of the compost with a light spray.

Germination can be very quick taking anything from 1 - 2 weeks. Once your seeds germinate, prize them out of the compost gently. Tip - always handle the seedlings by their leaves. Prepare some fresh compost in 2 - 3 inch pots and transfer each seedling into their own pot by planting them level with their own natural collar.

Water and label each pot and position them into bright shade. You should aim to plant the seedlings into their final garden position within 12 - 15 months by which time the seedlings should be at least 1 foot tall. If you need to in the interim period, continue to pot the seedlings up (always taking care not to disturb their roots).

Chapter 8) Health

Provided they are not overcrowded or kept in damp, stagnant conditions, stick insects are unlikely to become ill. If they do become ill, it is very difficult to tell. There are a few symptoms of illness that you will notice, due to their size and the infrequency of activity.

Stick insects are completely dependent on their owners to provide the correct accommodation and food. If they are given leaves that have been sprayed with pesticide they may die. If their home is too low and small they may not be able to climb out of their skins. If stick insects are not given enough space they may fight with and eat other stick insects that are being kept with them.

a) Poison

A stick insect that is twitching has probably eaten leaves that have been treated with pesticide and is likely to die. You need to make sure that any food plants you use don't have any pesticides on them. A quick rinse is always a good idea anyway.

b) Loosing legs

It may be very alarming, but loosing a leg is quite common for stick insects and it doesn't cause them too much distress. They often loose their legs for a variety of reasons but will happily survive with as few as three so long as they have one or more on each side.

Stick insects can lose limbs for a number of reasons and you should be careful to avoid any situation that may cause your stick insects to lose limbs. Some of the common causes of lost limbs include:

An unsuccessful moult. This can cause the leg or part of the leg to come off in the skin. To avoid this happening, make sure that you're keeping your stick insects at the right humidity.

One of my Lonchodes Philippinicus nymphs managed to leave one of her legs behind in the egg when she hatched over a month ago, but as you can see from the photograph, she is strong thriving!

They will often grow new legs with a moult anyway. There isn't much you can do in the way of hurrying this along or finding out if they will re-grow.

Overcrowding - the stick insects bite or knock off legs of other stick insects in their cage. Your stick insects should have plenty of room in their cage and this is especially important when they are moulting.

Fungal infection - if you suspect your stick insects have a fungal infection, thoroughly clean their cage and, if necessary, quarantine infected individuals.

Rough handling - stick insects are fragile and, like all animals, should be handled with care and respect.

c) Mould

If their cage is kept too damp, mould may grow and conditions can get unhealthy. It's difficult to keep the balance right, between nice and humid and warm and the perfect conditions for mould to thrive.

The main thing you can do to prevent mould growth is to be vigilant. If you keep a good eye out for the first signs of mould, you can usually wipe it away with no further worry.

If the mould is persistent, however, you should remove the insects to a temporary enclosure and treat the mould. Treat the mould with a weak solution of bleach and water mixed up in a plastic bottle. Spray it on, then wipe off. Or if you have time and somewhere suitable to keep your creepers overnight, add soda crystals to water and try soaking overnight for a more eco-friendly option without the pungent fumes! If you don't have soda crystals, use biological washing powder. Scrub any pesky bits of mould stuck in the hem or seams with a nailbrush. Make sure you rinse whatever you use off thoroughly, as it may damage the stick insects.

It is very important not to allow mould in the home, not just for the stick insects, but also for anyone else living in your home. Damp mould or mildew is an allergen and may increase health problems for asthma or hay fever sufferers, and even for people with no underlying conditions, too.

d) Drying out

One thing that can really mess up the long-term health of your stick insects is drying out. It's a difficult line to walk, between too wet and too dry, but the humidity needs of these creatures is given for a reason – dryness kills.

It can stop them hatching out properly. If the egg is too dry, the nymph can become trapped in the egg. Unable to move, eat, or drink, they will die in their eggs. Or they can part hatch. The part hatch is heartbreaking to behold, with the tiny little crawler pulling itself about on 2 or 4 legs, with the others stuck in the egg. If they can get out, and sometimes a little late spray can help with that, the back legs can be left damaged. If not they will soon die.

Being too dry can also stop the moult happening properly. This will mean that the stick insect is trapped inside its exoskeleton while it grows. It is stuck. The body is squashed inside its own protective shell and it is crushed to death. Not nice.

Drying out the food is also bad. The tiny little head and mouth of the stick insect, while strong for the size, can't cope well with dry, brittle and hard leaves. If they can bite through this, these leaves aren't good for the stick insect, and they will starve.

e) Hot

The heat you keep your phasmid on will depend on whom you're keeping. Some of them do like the heat, but even the most heat tolerant don't like too much. There are all sorts of horrid things that can happen with stick insects that overheat.

The most obvious is that they dry out. Drying out because of heat can have all the same consequences as drying out because of poor humidity.

They can also get heat exhaustion. The digestion will speed up beyond a useful point. The nutrition won't be absorbed. The cells will be damaged by too much exposure to heat and the insects will age quickly and their lifespan will be dramatically shortened.

f) Cold

Cold in stick insects, as with many animals, can cause a state called torpor. Torpor is a temporary state of suspension or sleep, during which the insect is completely immobile. This can be mistaken for death. Or it can kill them, if they don't come out of it properly.

The cold can make stick insects very lethargic. They get a lot of their energy from the temperature and cold can really slow them down. It slows down digestion so that they don't take as much nutrients as they need and it slows down movement so they can't get about very quickly. It also slows reactions so that if they fall they are more likely to get injured.

g) Moulting

As mentioned above, they grow by shedding their skin and to be able to do this they hang from the food plant or from the ceiling of their cage. They need room to moult properly. Insufficient space can cause them to develop deformities as their new skin hardens but often these will not affect their ability to survive.

Not moulting properly can make stick insects very ill. But a good moult can make your stick insects look all shiny and new.

It might seem creepy, but stick insects will shed their whole skin, including from the antennae. They leave little ghost like shells of themselves over the cage. These 3 moults are from the same stick insect over a 2-month period.

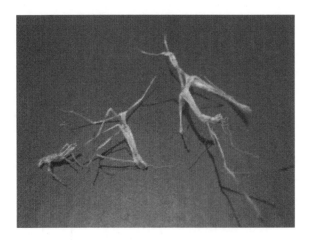

h) Growing/dwarfism

Insufficient food and water during growth can cause the segments of the body between the legs, the thorax, to be stunted. The body doesn't develop properly and the animal will not thrive and will normally die young.

To avoid this, you can need to make sure that as soon as the nymphs hatch they have enough food and that they can eat it.

i) Mites

Stick insects can suffer from mites, small, white creatures that will run about on their skin. Mites will bite and damage the stick insects. You brush them off gently and clean the enclosure thoroughly, replacing the food plants. Keep repeating this process once a day for 3 days after you can't see any mites, to stop them reoccurring.

j) Sudden unexpected death

If your stick insect dies you can usually work out why by asking yourself a few questions. Was it warm enough? Was it cool enough? Did it have enough ventilation? Did it have enough food? Did an aggressive species (yes, Mackleas, we're looking at you!) get in with it? Was there any mould in the tank? Was there enough/too much water? How old are they?

If you can't work out why, then remove the others, clean out the tank and replace all to food, just to be on the safe side. Because there has been so little research into pathogens that affect phasmids and there are no real reasons to find 'cures', this is all that you can do to stop the spread of unexpected deaths.

Chapter 9) Breeding

There is not just one way to breed phasmids successfully.
Breeding conditions that prove to be of value for one breeder
might not lead down the road of success for another breeder.
There is a very complex interplay of different environmental
factors at work when breeding phasmids, which vary greatly
from breeder to breeder. And this interplay is not really
understood - even by experienced breeders.

You need to make sure that the humidity and temperature are
perfect and that there is an abundance of food – animals that
aren't sure of their future food supply are less likely to
successfully breed. If they are in good health, though, you can
usually manage it, apart from with some of the trickier species.

a) Methods of reproduction

Some phasmids, like some lizards and plants, will reproduce by
parthenogenesis. This is a process by which growth and
development of embryos occur without fertilization. In animals,
parthenogenesis means development of an embryo from an
unfertilized egg cell.

Normal egg cells form after meiosis and are haploid, with half as
many chromosomes as their mother's body cells. Haploid
individuals, however, are usually non-viable, and
parthenogenetic offspring usually have the diploid chromosome
number. Depending on the mechanism involved in restoring the
diploid number of chromosomes, parthenogenetic offspring may

have anywhere between all and half of the mother's alleles. The offspring with all of the mother's genetic material are called full clones and those with only half are called "half clones". Full clones are usually formed without meiosis. If meiosis occurs, the offspring will get only a fraction of the mother's alleles.

Individuals born by parthenogenesis are usually all female.

Many species, though, reproduce using sexual reproduction, and the females need to be mated in order for the eggs to hatch.

b) Hatching eggs

Most breeders advise that you keep the eggs, nymphs and adults separately so as to keep everyone healthy. You should find and remove as many eggs as you can and place eggs on vermiculite, damp tissue or similar.

When you're hatching the eggs, if you spread some dried sphagnum moss over the eggs this will make it much easier for the nymphs to hatch safely and it also reduces mould growth to some extent.

They should be kept warm and damp, but clean and free from mould. Most eggs can be keep at room temperature of 20-25°C whereas others will need to be kept in a warm airing cupboard. You can buy vermiculite in some pet shops or from garden centres. You can also get it online.

Mist lightly every few days to keep the surroundings damp but not wet.

Check regularly for mould as if left to grow it will kill the nymphs inside.

Eggs generally take 4-6 months to hatch from being laid depending on temperature, although some species will hatch at only a month and others can take up to over a year!

Warmer temperatures will cause them to hatch sooner and cooler temperatures will take longer.

Some of the information below will have a "HH" beside the species. This is to indicate a type of incubation. HH incubation is very simple, and can really increase your chances of hatching the eggs.

Material needed:

A clear box with a tightly closing lid (like a takeaway box) some smaller plastic cups or boxes (about 2 cm lower than the plastic box!)
Fine stockings
thoroughly washed aquarium sand
some kitchen paper
Sphagnum moss

Put kitchen paper or a paper towel in the bigger box and make it really wet.

Cut a hole in the lid of the box. The hole in the lid serves as ventilation.

Make it just big enough to prevent condensation inside the box. Condensed water can be a death trap for freshly hatched nymphs, and it increases mould growth.

Cover the hole in the lid with a fine stocking, which will help freshly hatched nymphs to get a better grip when hanging below the lid.

Half fill the smaller plastic cup with sand - and put the eggs on top of the sand.

Place the sand-filled plastic cups with the eggs inside the bigger clear box - directly on the wet paper towel.

For eggs of species from rather dry areas or areas with a dry season, do not moisten the sand. The humidity of the air will be enough to ensure a healthy development of the eggs.

Spread some Sphagnum moss loosely over the eggs, this will help the nymphs on hatching a lot. Like this, almost no nymph will get stuck to the eggshell or be badly damaged.

The small cup can be closed with netting, if it contains eggs of a small species. This might be helpful when eggs of different species are incubated in the same box and the appearance of the hatching nymphs is not known.

If the cup contains eggs of rather big or very big species, then leave the cup open. This should give enough space for the big nymphs and only few will be damaged by the cramped space.

84

The most important thing in breeding your stick insects is the eggs. Keep the eggs clean and humid and they should be fine.

c) Species specific breeding

Heteropteryx dilatata (HH)

Females are born a beige colour, which fades as it moults, while the male is a darker brown. This species produces sexually and breeds well, with the females being very receptive for most of the year.

The female will deposit the dark, round eggs in moist soil. The eggs take from 12 to 14 months to hatch.

Acrophylla Wuelfingi

The Acrophylla Wuelfingi breeds well; with the females starting to lay eggs 3 weeks after the last moult. When hatched young they are 1 inch (2.5cm) long, light green with red eyes. They are rather fragile during the first instar. They should be kept at 22-23°C. They are sexual. The eggs incubate for 3-4 month at 20-25°C, 70% humidity.

Neophasma subapterum (HH)

This is a very easy species to breed, 80-90% of the eggs hatch. This happens after 3-5 months. The eggs are produced sexually. Keep them humid on vermiculite, mist every three days.

Once matured, females can lay over 30 eggs a week, which, if kept in the correct condition, will hatch with a very high success rate.

This species requires a male to fertilise the eggs.

Eggs will be dropped to the bottom of the cage.

Achrioptera

All of the Achrioptera require a lot of light. If you have the space, then put their cage right in front of a window with some direct morning sun. But make sure that the sun cannot heat the cage up too much.

Achrioptera punctipes cliquennoisi

This subspecies is very difficult to breed successfully, and very few people have managed it. The eggs, if you manage to get any, are very large and have a brown to green colour with dark brown texturing. They will often seem cracked, though this doesn't seem to affect the hatch rate.

They are quite big when they do hatch out, so you need to make sure there will be room for them when they arrive.

One thing to be aware of with this species is that you shouldn't keep more males than females in the cage, as they tend to pester the females.

Achrioptera Fallax (HH)

The Achrioptera Fallax is the easiest of the Achrioptera to breed. The eggs are smaller than those of the Punctipes Punctipes and punctipes cliquennoisi at 5-6mm long and only 2mm wide.

Achrioptera Punctipes Punctipes

These are easier to breed than the punctipes cliquennoisi, but it's still not going to be easy. You should keep them together and they do the rest themselves. The difficulty here is getting the eggs to hatch.

Acrophylla Wuflfingi (HH)

The large Acrophylla Wuflfingi breeds easily with the large, round eggs laid on the floor of the cage.

Diapherodes Gigantea

The large eggs of this species are easy to hatch, as long as they are not too wet or too dry. Females will start to lay at 4 weeks and she will lay about 20 eggs a week; over half of these should hatch given the correct conditions.

Borneo Giant Thorny Stick Insects (HH)

These stick insects usually reproduce sexually, though they can reproduce by parthenogenesis. Eggs laid without fertilization take up to nine months to hatch and produce only females. Eggs produced sexually will hatch sooner and produce both males and females. In either cases, the female "flicks" her eggs, swinging her tail, up to several feet to land on the forest floor.

Parapachymorpha zomproi

Parapachymorpha zomproi don't lay too many eggs, so you won't end up overrun. With the right conditions they will breed happily. The eggs can be hatched in a container on damp tissue in a warm place. Check a couple of times a week to keep them from getting mouldy or drying out.

Extatosoma Tiaratum (HH)

These stick insects usually reproduce sexually, though they can reproduce by parthenogenesis. Eggs laid without fertilization take up to nine months to hatch and produce only females. Eggs produced sexually will hatch sooner and produce both males and females.

In either cases, the female "flicks" her eggs, swinging her tail, up to several feet to land on the forest floor. Unlike most stick insects, these eggs must be kept relatively cool - under 25°C - or they are unlikely to hatch.

Phaenopharos Khaoyaiensis

These phasmids don't need males to reproduce, they use parthenogenesis. They breed well with the right conditions. The round, black eggs will hatch in 4-6 months and will only need a damp paper towel to hatch on. They don't need soil to lay in.

Ramulus nematodes Blue

This is such an easy species to breed, as long as you make sure that your Ramulus nematodes are from the same place, as they can sometimes fail to breed if they aren't 'local' to each other.

The eggs are 6mm long and thin, brown lumpy things that look like wildflower seeds.

You should keep the nymphs in smaller cages and transfer them to bigger cages –appropriate to their size – as they grow bigger. Too much space can stress them.

Peruphasma schultei

These little beauties are easy to breed at room temperature, with the eggs even managing to hatch if they are dry. They are just spot on! As long as they are kept well fed and not too humid, the Peruphasma schultei will breed very happily in humidity.

Neohiasea maerens (HH)

The Neohiasea maerens reproduce sexually, so you need males and females to mate, as only mated eggs are fertile. The eggs are 2mm ovals and are dark grey/brown in colour. They hatch well on damp paper towels kept in an airing cupboard or on a small heat mat, with over half of them hatching in the right conditions. They can take 4-8 months to hatch.

Asceles

This species lays strangely. The female will lay the eggs actually in a leaf. They cut holes in the leaf and lay them there. You shouldn't remove them from the leaves they are laid on, as this can damage the case of the egg. You can leave the eggs in with the adults.

Heteropteryx dilatata

These aggressive little things breed readily with good conditions. They breed sexually, so you need to keep males and females in together. They lay 20-30 eggs a week from 4 months old. The eggs take up to 14 months to hatch.

Longhodes Philippinicus

The Longhodes Philippinicus breeds well, and the female needs a substrate to lay in. Coconut coir works well for this. They lay 20-30 eggs a week and they lay from 4 months old.

Xenophasmina (HH)

The Xenophasmina are easy to breed with a high hatch rate. The eggs are about 4.5mm by 2.5mm and have a bumpy surface. This species breeds from 4-5 months old. If the males and females are kept together in even numbers and their living conditions are good enough, they will happily breed.

A female will lay about 30 eggs a week, and over half of them will hatch, if kept properly. They should be kept on slightly damp sand at room temperature.

Mearnsiana Bullosa (HH)

The eggs of this species are 5mm by 3mm and a dark, grey/brown colour. They will breed at 4 months and eggs will be laid in clutches of about 30. Eggs will be laid in substrate. The females become very distressed if they can't find substrate to lay in. It's best to provide dry sand to lay in, as this is easy to sieve the eggs from. They'll lay once every 2 or 3 weeks.

Lopaphus Magnificus

The Lopaphus Magnificus has small, oval eggs, and lots of them. They breed easily and well, with the right conditions you can end up with far too many nymphs. Luckily, as they are very pretty when they are adults, you can usually trade, swap or sell the nymphs of the Lopaphus Magnificus quite easily.

Cranidium Gibbosum

The Cranidium Gibbosum will happily breed if they have enough food. They will breed from about 4-5 months old.

They will lay 20-30 eggs a week, of which about half will hatch given the right conditions. They need to be kept on slightly damp sand.

Eurycantha Calcarata

Keeping the males and females in the same cage is all you really need to do to get them to mate.

The eggs are small, light brown ovals, which are deposited in the ground. The ovipositor of the female is used to "drill" a hole in the ground where the egg is laid into. She will then use her ovipositor to bury the egg by sweeping soil over the just drilled hole.

The eggs hatch after about 4 to 6 months. The eggs should be kept in moist soil. This should always remain moist but not extremely wet.

Tirachoidea Jianfenglingensis

This is a very easy species to breed, given the correct conditions. You need males and females to breed these successfully. They can breed from about 4 months.

The females will lay 30-40 eggs a week and over 50% of these should hatch. These don't want wet sand, but a damp paper towel and some sphagnum moss will do wonders.

Pharnacia kirbyi

This is a very easy species to breed, with the large eggs having a high hatch rate and the males reaching maturity at 3 months, whereas the females reach it at 4. They will mate readily and lay all over the floor! The incubation time at room temperatures is about 4 months and the hatching rate is usually over half.

You should really think twice about trying to hatch these, though, as the adults take up a lot of room, and can be difficult to re-home. But if you can find people on forums that are interested before you hatch any, then you could give it a go.

Chapter 10) Stick and leaf insects in education

There is so much you can do with phasmids in the classroom. They are useful for behavioural, aesthetic and developmental observations. Phasmids are good to look at as classifications too, as they have easy to distinguish features. You can also use them over time to look at food pyramids.

Behaviour

You can do a few experiments with stick insects to find out about their behaviour. This is a great experiment. If you can get 2 different types of phasmid that eat different foods you can keep them in separate cages and do a comparison too!

Food

Place different food plants in the cage with the stick insects, bramble and privet and whatever food your stick insects eat, and some other plants. The students can keep tables and make notes about the food that is eaten. They might even be able to do a Venn diagram of the foods that the 2 types eat and don't eat. For example, X eats this, Y eats this and the both eat this. Or X won't eat this, Y won't eat this and neither will eat this.

Temp

For this experiment you'll need a few little cages. Make sure that the stick insects in each cage are the same age and species.

Place one near the window, one on your desk (or somewhere of average temperature) and one near the radiator or on a heat mat. Make sure they all have the same amount of food and the right humidity. Then compare how well they are doing over time. A good way to do this is to observe movement and growth rate.

The students could do a bar chart of the 3 cages, showing the average length of the stick insects each week. This experiment may result in some fatalities, though, so you need to keep an eye out. If any of the cold stick insects start to get torpid (sleepy and sluggish) move them to somewhere warmer. You also need to make sure that the hot stick insects are humid enough.

Ventilation

Stick insects need ventilation. Different species need different amounts of ventilation. You can do a long-term experiment about ventilation. Keep the stick insects in differently ventilated cages and see which ones do best. A good indicator of a happy stick insect is eggs. If they breed, then they are thriving.

Development

You can use stick insects as a great tool to observe development. As stick insects grow and change, students can document their developments.

Size

By measuring the length of the phasmids, students can draw graphs and tables of their length. They might also be able to weigh them, but you'd need very sensitive scales to do this!

Colour

As stick insects grow, change and eventually moult, they change colour. When nymphs hatch, their primary goal is not to be seen and eaten. Getting older, their priorities change, and attracting a mate is often up highest.

For this you might need more interesting coloured insects than the common Indian stick insect. The students can make a colour chart of the changes as the stick insects change colour, from the almost black hatchlings to their adult colours.

Male or female?

Students can compare the difference between males and females as they grow and develop. You can do all of the observations above and compare the males to the females.

Classification

Using strips of card or paper, make a list of animals (to make it as varied as you can include mammals, fish, insects, birds, creepy crawlies etc). Then separate out those that have jointed legs. This should include insects and other animals. Next, separate out the animals that have exoskeletons. These are what we call arthropods – including both insects and spiders – and this is the family group that stick insects belong to.

You can get animal classifications sheets on the Internet.

Food pyramids

You can do great stuff with food pyramids using stick insects. You can work out (roughly) how much food is needed to keep them alive over a set period of time. When you decide to start this experiment, the stick insects should be nymphs, not fully grown, but big enough so that handling won't hurt them. To weigh the stick insects, first weigh a container and then put all of the stick insects in the container. Can the children work out how much the stick insects weight? Then weigh the food before it goes in to the cage and when it gets thrown out. Can the children work out how much as been eaten? Do this every time you change the food for a couple of weeks. Make this total weight the bottom of the pyramid. Then weigh the stick insects again, (assuming none have died!). Can the children work out how much weight they've put on? This is the next level of the pyramid.

Chapter 11) Biology

Phasmid bodies are made up of a thorax in 3 segments, a head, and a tail. The segmented thorax has a pair of legs on each section.

Stick and leaf insects have leathery, elongate bodies, and long, thin legs designed for walking slowly.

Leaf insect bodies tend to be flatter, with a horizontal surface that mimics a leaf, having curling, cut away edges to make them look more realistic.

Stick insects, like many other insects, have a growth cycle known as incomplete metamorphosis. This is where the adult and the nymph are very similar. The disadvantage of this is that both nymph and adult often share the same food source. Therefore they can be in direct competition with one another for food. The advantage is that the vulnerable pupa (chrysalis) phase is avoided. The wings develop during the nymph stages as wing buds. These grow larger at each successive instar. They are fully formed at the final moult into adulthood. This type of life cycle is seen in various insects, including dragonflies, grasshoppers, earwigs, cockroaches and true bugs (insects with sucking mouth parts).

Reproduction

The external male organs appear as relatively small projections below segments 8 and 9. Females possess an ovipositor, a larger structure from which the eggs are pushed out. The ovipositor consists of appendages from the 8th and 9th segments concealed by a flap-like plate, the operculum, which is derived from the lower covering of the 8th segment. These differences in shape can be useful in determining the gender of individual specimens.

In both sexes, there is a pair of un-segmented appendages arising from the rear of the abdomen called the cerci (singular: cercus). These may be involved in the mating process. In some species, eggs are fertilised in the conventional manner by male insects that are similar, although often smaller and differently coloured, to the female.

Both males and females may mate several times, the male standing on the back of the female and tucking his abdomen around and underneath hers. At this point, he may use his cerci to grip the female's abdomen. He then transfers sperm to the tip of the abdomen of the female in a small packet called a spermatophore. Sometimes, especially in larger species, the spermatophore falls to the bottom of the cage after mating. Normally, however, it remains attached to the female and sperm travel from it to a storage compartment at the tip of the female's abdomen. There the sperm are stored until eggs are produced. Sperm penetrate the eggs as they pass by the storage chamber en route to the outside world. This can mean that some species of stick insect only need to be mated once.

In some species, including the Indian stick insect, females regularly produce fertile eggs without the need for fertilisation by a male, a process known as parthenogenesis. Unsurprisingly, in these types, males are rare. In other species, fertilisation is usually conventional but parthenogenesis is possible in the absence of fertile male insects. Eggs are most commonly laid singly and dropped or flicked onto the ground. The females of a few species deposit their eggs in loose soil while others glue their eggs individually or in batches to leaves or branches.

Antennae

The antennae are a pair of sense organs located near the front of an insect's head capsule. Although commonly called "feelers", the antennae are much more than just tactile receptors. They are usually covered with olfactory receptors that can detect odour molecules in the air (the sense of smell).

Many insects also use their antennae as humidity sensors, to detect changes in the concentration of water vapour. Stick insects have a pair of simple, filament-like antennae, which in some cases can be quite long. Males usually have longer antennae than females. All phasmids have lengthy segmented antennae, with anywhere from 8 to 100 segments depending on the species.

Mouth

All Phasmids feed on foliage, and possess chewing mouthparts designed for breaking down plant material. These mouthparts are forward facing and designed to bite off pieces of leaf. They consist of an upper lip (the labrum), a lower lip (labium), a pair of jaws (mandibles) to chop the food and a pair of secondary jaws (maxillae). The labium and maxillae bear sensory palps to taste the food and move it towards the mouth.

Eyes

All phasmids possess compound eyes, but ocelli are only found in some winged males. Phasmids have an impressive visual system that allows them to perceive significant detail even in dim conditions, which suits their typically nocturnal lifestyle. They are born equipped with tiny compound eyes with a limited number of facets. As the insect grows through successive moults, the number of facets is increased along with the number of photoreceptor cells in the eye.

The sensitivity of the adult eye is at least tenfold that of the first instar nymphs. As the eye grows more complex, the mechanisms to adapt to dark/light changes are also enhanced: eyes in dark conditions show less screening pigments, which would block light, than during the daytime, and changes in the width of the retinal layer to adapt to changes in available light are significantly more pronounced in adults.

However, the larger size of the adult insects' eyes makes them more prone to radiation damage. This explains why fully-grown individuals are mostly nocturnal. Lessened sensitivity to light in the newly emerged insects helps them to escape from the leaf litter wherein they are hatched and move upward into the illuminated foliage.

Thorax

The thorax has three segments called (from the head end) the pro-thorax, meso-thorax and meta-thorax. Each bears a similar pair of legs, although the rear pair may be somewhat larger and stronger. The end section of each leg consists of five parts called tarsi (singular – tarsus).

Pro-thorax

The pro-thorax is the short, first segment of the thorax. The fore legs are attached to this segment. The head of the stick insect comes from the front of the pro-thorax, and the longer meso-thorax is attached at the back.

Meso-thorax

The meso-thorax is a longer segment than the pro-thorax. It has another pair of legs and if the stick phasmid has wings, a pair of them will grow on the meso-thorax.

Meta-thorax

The last part of the thorax, the meta-thorax, has the last legs attached to it. If the stick insect has wings, the larger pair will be on the back here.

Spines

Some stick and leaf insects sport elaborate spines or other accessories, to improve their mimicry of plants. These spines can also act as defence, to help them avoid predators and to hurt anything that will bite them, or pick them up, in their little simian hands.

Legs

The legs come off during moulting, a process referred to as autotomy. This mechanism allows the insect to escape, capture or entangle with minimum damage, since a replacement limb grows and enlarges each time a moult occurs. The tarsi of regenerated legs are 4- rather than 5-segmented.

Abdomen

Despite appearances, there are eleven abdominal segments. The first or 'median' segment is closely linked to the metathorax, while the eleventh merely consists of a few projections attached to the last obvious abdominal segment. The 'median' segment is often important in classifying phasmids.

Wings

Most insects, at some point in their evolution, had wings. This is true of phasmids too. The meso and meta thorax both have a pair of wings. However, the wings are reduced or lost in some species, especially the females. The fore wings and the front portion of the hind wings are modified to cover and protect the folded, flying part of the hind wings. Flying is possible in some species but is never strong and usually consists of a fluttering glide. The wings of stick insects, because of the way they grow in an incomplete metamorphosis, develop outside the body and are said to be exopterygote.

Defence

Most species of stick and leaf insect show mechanisms for defence from predators that both prevent an attack from happening in the first place (primary defence) and are deployed after an attack has been initiated (secondary defence).

The defence mechanism most readily identifiable with Phasmids is camouflage, in the form of plant mimicry, which a lot of them are very good at. Most phasmids are known for effectively replicating the forms of sticks and leaves, and the bodies of some species are covered in mossy or lichen-like growths that supplement their disguise. Some species have the ability to change colour as their surroundings shift. In a further behavioural adaptation to supplement crypsis, a number of species perform a rocking motion where the body is swayed from side to side; this is thought to mimic the movement of leaves or twigs swaying in the breeze. Another method by which stick insects avoid predation and resemble twigs is by feigning death, where the insect enters a motionless state that can be maintained for a long period. The nocturnal feeding habits of adults also help Phasmatodea to remain concealed from predators.

In a seemingly opposite method of defence, many species of Phasmatodea seek to startle the encroaching predator by flashing bright colours that are normally hidden, and making a loud noise. When disturbed on a branch or foliage, some species, while dropping to the undergrowth to escape, will open their wings momentarily during free fall to display bright colours that disappear when the insect lands. Others will maintain their display for up to 20 minutes, hoping to frighten the predator and convey the appearance of a larger size. Some accompany the visual display with noise made by rubbing together parts of the wings or antennae.

Some species, such as the young nymphs of Extatosoma tiaratum, have been observed to curl the abdomen upwards over the body and head to resemble ants or scorpions in an act of mimicry, another defence mechanism by which the insects avoid becoming prey.

When threatened, some phasmids that are equipped with femoral spines on the legs on the meta thorax respond by curling the abdomen upward and repeatedly swinging the legs together, grasping at the threat. If the menace is caught, the spines can draw blood and inflict considerable pain.

A number of species are equipped with a pair of glands at the anterior edge of the pro-thorax that enables the insect to release defensive secretions, including chemical compounds of varying effect: from the production of distinct odours to the causing of a stinging, burning sensation in the eyes and mouth of a predator. The spray often contains pungent-smelling, volatile metabolites, previously thought to be concentrated in the insect from its plant food sources. However, based on recent research, it seems more likely that they manufacture their own chemical defence substances.

Additionally, the chemistry of the defence spray from at least one species, *Anisomorpha buprestoides*, has been shown to vary, based on their life stage and/or population. This chemical spray variation also corresponds with regionally specific colour form populations in Florida, which also have distinct behaviours. The spray from one species, *Megacrania nigrosulfurea*, is used as a treatment for skin infections by a tribe in Papua New Guinea because of its antibacterial constituents. Some species employ a shorter-range defensive secretion, where individuals bleed reflexively through the joints of their legs and the seams of the exoskeleton when bothered, allowing the blood (hemolymph), which contains distasteful additives, to discourage predators. Stick insects, like their distant relative the grasshopper, can also discharge the contents of their stomachs through vomiting when harassed, a fluid considered inedible by some predators.

Life cycle

The life cycle of the stick insect begins when the female deposits her eggs through one of these methods of oviposition: she will either flick her egg to the ground by a movement of the ovipositor or her entire abdomen, carefully place the eggs in the axils of the host plant, bury them in small pits in the soil, or stick the eggs to a substrate, usually a stem or leaf of the food plant. A single female lays from 100 to 1,200 eggs after mating, depending on the species.

Many species of phasmids are parthenogenic, meaning the females lay eggs without needing to mate with males to produce offspring. Stick insect species that are the product of hybridisation are usually obligate parthenogens, but non-hybrids are facultative parthenogens, meaning they retain the ability to mate and are bisexual depending on the presence and abundance of males. Eggs from virgin mothers are entirely female and exact copies of their mothers.

Phasmatodea eggs resemble seeds in shape and size, and have hard shells. They have a lid-like structure called an operculum at the anterior pole, from which the nymph emerges during hatching. The eggs vary in the hatching period, from 13 to more than 70 days, with the average around 20–30 days. Some species, particularly those from temperate regions, undergo diapauses, where development is delayed during the winter months. Diapause is affected by photoperiod on the egg-laying adults or can be genetically determined. Diapause is broken by exposure to the cold of winter, causing the eggs to hatch during the following spring. Among species of economic importance, diapause affects the development of two-year cycles of outbreaks.

Many species' eggs bear a fatty, knoblike capitulum that caps the operculum. This structure attracts ants because of its resemblance to the elaiosome, or seed, of some plant seeds that are sought-after food sources for ant larvae, and usually contribute to ensuring seed dispersal by ants, a form of ant-plant mutualism called myrmecochory. The ants take the egg into their nest underground and can remove the capitulum to feed to their larvae without harming the phasmid embryo. There, the egg hatches and the young nymph, which initially resembles an ant (another instance of mimicry among Phasmatodea), eventually emerges from the nest and climbs the nearest tree to safety in the foliage.

The Phasmatodea life cycle is hemimetabolous, proceeding through a series of several instars when they are just still nymphs. The stick insect's wings develop externally. As is the case with hatching, if the nymph is caught in the encasing of a rejected cast skin (or shell), it will likely die because it cannot free itself. Once emerged, the nymphs will eat the cast skin. Adulthood is reached for most species after several months and many moults. The lifespan of Phasmatodea varies by species, but ranges from a few months to up to two years for some tropical varieties.

Endangered

Little is known about stick insects, making it difficult to declare the vulnerability of their status in the wild. The pet trade presents a potential threat. There are a great many phasmids on the endangered species list, and their numbers are growing.

The Australian Lord Howe Island stick insect was thought to be completely extinct, until recently. Now that they have been rediscovered, as they were in 2001, they are part of a captive breeding program. The Lord Howe Island looks like a long, black cockroach, almost like a scorpion. But despite their ugly countenance, they are a vital part of their environment and should be protected and celebrated - they've come back, from the brink of extinction.

Behaviour

Stick insects, like praying mantises, show rocking behaviour in which the insect makes rhythmic, repetitive, side-to-side movements. The common interpretation of this behaviour's function is that it enhances crypsis by mimicking vegetation moving in the wind. However, these movements may be most important in allowing the insects to discriminate objects from the background by relative motion – it may help them determine distances! Rocking movements by these generally sedentary insects may replace flying or running as a source of relative motion to help them discern objects in the foreground.

Mating behavior in Phasmatodea is impressive because of the extraordinarily long duration of pairings. A record among insects, the stick insect *Necroscia sparaxes*, found in India, is sometimes coupled for 79 days at a time. It is not uncommon for this species to assume the mating posture for days or weeks on end, and among some species (*Diapheromera veliei and D. Covilleae*), pairing has been observed to last three to 136 hours in captivity. Explanations for this behaviour range from males guarding their mates against reproductive competitors to the view that the pairings are a defensive alliance.

Instances of overt displays of aggression between males over mates would suggest the extended pairing behaviour might have evolved to guard females against sperm competition. Fighting between competing males has been observed in the species *D. veiliei* and *D. covilleae*. During these encounters, the approach of a challenger causes the existing mate to manipulate the female's abdomen, which he has clasped by means of the clasping organ, or vomer, down upon itself to block the site of attachment. Occasionally, the consort will strike out at the competitor with the mid femora, which are equipped with an enlarged and hooked spine in both sexes that has been observed to draw the blood of the opponent when they are flexed against the body to puncture the integument.

Usually, a strong hold on the female's abdomen and blows to the intruder are enough to deter the unwanted competition, but occasionally the competitor has been observed to employ a sneaky tactic to inseminate the female. While the first mate is engaged in feeding and is forced to vacate the dorsal position, the intruder can clasp the female's abdomen and insert his genitalia. If he is discovered, the males will enter into combat wherein they lean backward, both clasped to the female's abdomen, and freely suspended, engage in rapid, sweeping blows with their forelegs in a manner similar to boxing. Usually, when the intruder gains attachment to the female's abdomen, these conflicts resolve in the displacement of the original mate.

Lengthy pairings have also been described in terms of a defensive alliance. When cleaved together, the pair is more unwieldy for predators to handle. Also, the chemical defences (secretions, reflex bleeding, regurgitation) of the individual stick insect are enhanced when two are paired. Female survivorship of attacks by predators is significantly enhanced by pairing, largely because the dorsal position of the male functions well as a shield. This could indicate manipulation by females is present: if females accept ejaculate at a slow rate, for instance, the males are forced to remain *in copulo* for longer and the female's chances of survival are enhanced. Also, evolution could have simply favoured males that remained attached to their females longer, since females are often less abundant than males and represent a valuable prize, so for the lucky male, even the

110

sacrifice of his own life to preserve his offspring with the female may be worth it.

Sexual dimorphism in the species, where females are usually significantly larger than the males, may have evolved due to the fitness advantage accrued to males that can remain attached to the female, thereby blocking competitors, without severely impeding her movement.

Reference websites

http://www.freewebs.com/christiemay3/stickinsectsforsale.htm
http://www.cleapss.org.uk/attachments/article/0/L227.pdf?Primar
y/Resources/Guides/
www.virginiacheeseman.co.uk

Index

Printed in Great Britain
by Amazon